THE BOOK OF
DUBLINMAN
JOKES

by

Y. M. HUGHES

MERCIER PRESS

MERCIER PRESS
PO Box 5, 5 French Church Street, Cork
16 Hume Street, Dublin 2

Trade enquiries to CMD DISTRIBUTION,
55a Spruce Avenue, Stillorgan Industrial Park, Blackrock, Dublin

ISBN 0 85342 488 8

14 13 12 11 10 9 8 7 6 5

Printed in Ireland by Colour Books Ltd.

This book is humpily dedicated to

Herself and the kids, the Woman next door, my PP, TD, HEO, DJ, HP, JC, OS, QT, VG, TT and YR, the J's, the CB's, Michael D, John B, John D, all my friends and relations on The Arts Council, Peigín Leitir Mór, the Milkman, the Banim Bros, all the O'Briens (William Smith, Conor Cruise and Johnston Mooney Ando), Federick Foresight, The Washerwoman's Hill Society, Kitty the Hare, Mary the Pill, Fr Peter and Caoch O'Leary, Culchies everywhere, the Goatstown Bus, Mickeo, Little Liam, Big Tom, Mother Ireland, Lady Morgan, the Walls of Limerick, the Rocks of Cashel, the Bridges of Athlone, the Rakes of Mallow, Instant Spuds, all the Halls (Frank, Carnegie and Fr Matthew), Big Benjy, Neely the Fiddler, Terence the Veer, Charlotte Bronte, Oliver the Gun, An Pilibín Ultach, Ian the Mouth, Pogue Mahoney, Speedy Gonzales, B. McGrew, Dirty Nellie, Handy Andy, The Twangman's Ball, Johnny Guiles LP, Desperate Dan, Liam Ó Morocco, Mary Mear, Gráinne Mhaol and begrudgers everywhere.

Yorry Hughes

The taxi crawled along Dame Street in Dublin in heavy traffic, much to the annoyance of the passenger.

PASSENGER: 'Can't you go any faster, driver?'

DUBLIN TAXI DRIVER: 'Yes, sir, but I'm not allowed to leave the cab.'

*   *   *

Dublin man, out for a stroll in Dollymount, comes across a lone golfer unsuccessfully trying to hack his way out of a bunker. He watches him for some time in silence and then feels he must offer some help. So he shouts to the golfer, 'You can stop hitting now, it's dead.'

*   *   *

Lot's wife looked back and turned into a pillar of salt. Dublin lady driver looked back and turned into a bollard.

*   *   *

What did the Dublinman say after his cat was run over by a steamroller? Nothing. He just stood there with a long puss.

*   *   *

Little Audrey went into the chemist's shop and noticed the floor was wet.

LITTLE AUDREY: 'What is that on the floor?'

CHEMIST: 'It is H_2O.'

But little Audrey laughed and laughed. She knew it was K_9P.

*   *   *

GUEST (to lift-man outside penthouse suite in Gresham): 'Why do you keeping calling me "Son"?'

LIFT-MAN: 'I brought you up, didn't I?'

*   *   *

Two Howth herrings in a school of fish. Teacher asks one where his brother is.

'I must explain,' answered the herring, 'that I am not my brother's kipper.'

*   *   *

A man, jailed for twenty years kept his sanity by befriending an ant that used to share his cell. He even made a two-storey home for him in a matchbox. To while away the hours the convict made a tiny guitar and in five years he taught the ant to sing and play the guitar. In the long winter evenings the ant was of great consolation, giving recitals and concerts for his benefactor.

In another few years the convict had taught the ant to dance and by his twelfth year he was also an accomplished uilleann pipe player.

As the day of his release approached the convict began to realise that he had in his possession the greatest television performer ever know. He would be rich, famous . . .

On the day of their release the ex-convict rushed to the nearest pub to celebrate his liberty. He ordered a pint and while he drank it he produced the matchbox, shook the ant onto the counter of the deserted bar and asked for a tune. The ant rose to the occasion with a lovely rendition of *The Heart Bowed Down*. He was powerful. His owner, so overcome with joy, calls over the barman and nods towards the ant.

'What d'ye think of that?' sez he.

Whereupon the barman raises his hand, brings it down on the counter and kills the ant.

'Sorry about that, sir,' sez he, 'it's the hot weather.'

*　　*　　*

A spinster lady from Greystones always kept her foulmouthed parrot covered on Sunday morning when the parish priest called round for a sherry. Each Sunday morning for years she would rush for the cover when she heard the P.P. approach. One Sunday the parish priest departed leaving his umbrella behind him. An hour later he returned and it was the mercy of God that the spinster recognised him through the frosted glass of the hall door. She rushed in, covered the cage, opened the door and greeted her guest.

He did not linger but collected his brolly and went home.

With a sigh of relief she walked into the parlour. As she removed the cover from the cage she overheard the parrot saying to himself, 'That was an effin short week!'

* * *

They met in the revolving door of the G.P.O. and went round for ages together.

* * *

'Why do you call him "Button B"?'
'He seems always to be pressed for money.'

*　*　*

'It's bloody cold in bed these nights.'
'Why don't you buy one of those convector heaters?'
'Git outa that, sure there's hardly room in the bed for meself and the missus.'

*　*　*

QUIZMASTER on cookery programme: 'Should chips be eaten with the fingers?' CULCHIE: 'Noa! The fingers should be eaten separately.'

*　*　*

When Cearbhall Ó Dálaigh was President of Ireland he visited Rutland Street and spent some time talking to the children.

'And what are you going to be?' he asked one hardy wee lad.

'A lollipop-man, sir,' came the reply.

'Why a lollipop-man?' enquired the President.

'Yeh don't start till you're 65,' said the child.

*　*　*

Two culchies from north of Drumcondra were crossing a bridge over the river Dodder. There was this fella leaning over the parapet so, being culchies, they followed suit. Only then did they notice that he was holding a girl by the ankles whose head and shoulders were in the water.

'What are y'at?' sez a culchie.

'We are fishing,' sez the well-spoken Dublin man.

'How could you fish like that?' sez your man.

'Well,' sez the Dublin man, 'the mott here waits for a fish to pass by. As it passes she tickles its tummy, giving a slight jerk of her left leg as she does so. I pull her up quickly and there she is with a fish.

The culchies thought that here was another bloody Jackeen having them on but, even as they thought, the girl's ankle twitches and up she comes clutching a big brown trout to her bosom.

The culchies are amazed. Nothing will do them but to go into business for themselves. They rush off, find a bridge and one quickly lowers the other over the side.

In no time the pendent culchie's leg twitches and his butty roars out: 'Have yeh a fish?'

'No,' gurgles the other, 'there's a bloody train coming.'

* * *

Some of the residents of Ringsend live so close to the Liffey that their gardens open on to the river. They pride themselves on having ferries at the bottom of their garden.

* * *

Indeed, one Ringsend father, wondering what he should do with his son, had the sea planned for him. Fortunately the son managed to get out of the sack.

* * *

They stop outside his place on the way home from a dance.
HE: 'Well, how about a gin and platonic?'
WISE DOLLY-BIRD: 'And when we get inside you find out you've nothing but whiskey and sofa.'

* * *

'The brother got seven years for something he didn't do.'

'How did he manage that?'

'He didn't wipe his prints off the safe door.'

* * *

CORPORATION INSPECTOR: 'When did you realise that the roof was leaking?' DUBLIN CORPORATION TENANT: 'D'other day at dinner. It took me nearly three hours to drink me soup.'

* * *

Four over-worked priests, taking time off from duties which included seeing too much sickness and death, were having a quiet game of cards. All of a sudden one of them dropped dead.

'My God,' said a neighbour the following day, 'what was your immediate reaction.'

'Why, we took out the twos, threes and fours,' replied the cleric.

* * *

Two Dublin men talking about the proposed re-introduction of capital punishment.

JEM: 'I heard that in China they never hang a man with a long moustache.'

JOXER: 'Sure, I know. It 'id on'y break.'

* * *

There was this fella went to the Zoological Gardens commonly called the Azoo. He got chatting with one of the attendants and asked him if there was any chance of getting work there. 'Tell yeh what,' sez the attendant, 'the chimp dropped dead and if you'd like to put on that chimp suit and take his place you'll get a tenner a day.'

Well, your man, thinking a tenner wasn't to be sneezed at, decided to have a go, donned the chimp suit and got into the cage. He was an immediate success. His antics drew crowds around his cage leaving the lions in the next cage looking very dejected.

He was roaring and showing off on his trapeze when the gate adjoining the next cage burst open and in walks the biggest lion he had even seen. Your man in the chimp suit loses his nerve completely and roars for the keeper to come and let him out.

Suddenly the lion springs at him, lands on his back and knocks him to the ground. As the menacing jaws come close to his ear he hears the lion say, 'Shut up, for God's sake, or you'll get us both the sack.'

* * *

A fella goes to confession in Adam and Eve's.

PENITENT: 'I stole a length of material outa the job, father.'

FRANCISCAN: 'I hope you won't make a habit of it, my son.'

PENITENT: 'Well, no father—there's only enough in it for a suit.'

* * *

A little man tip-toes up O'Connell Street, stopping at intervals to scatter some kind of powder here and there on the street from a bag in his hand. His behaviour is so odd that he soon attracts a crowd of followers. A garda lurking in a door-way decides to investigate and approaches the man.

'What's in that bag?' says the lawman.

14

'Woffle dust,' sez the little man.

'What's that?' asks the Garda.

'Woffle dust is my own discovery,' sez your man, 'and is for the eradication of most varieties of poisonous snake.'

'But there are no snakes in O'Connell Street,' explains the garda.

'I know,' sez the little man. 'This is pretty powerful stuff.'

*   *   *

A horse dropped dead in Clanbrassil Street and a garda came to investigate. He produced his notebook and proceeded to take particulars. Being unable to spell Clanbrassil Street he had the drayman drag the horse around the corner so he could write 'Horse dropped dead in Patrick Street.'

*   *   *

YOUNG FELLA: 'Goin' inta town?'

SECOND YOUNG FELLA: 'Yea.'

YOUNG FELLA: 'Takin' a bus?'

SECOND YOUNG FELLA: 'No. Every time I take one me oul' wan makes me put it back.'

*   *   *

To protect his precious pint on the bar counter while he goes to the buckets, Dublin man scribbles a note and leaves it beside the glass: 'I have spit in this pint.'

When he returns to his drink he notices an addition to his note which reads: 'So have I.'

*   *   *

'She buried her husband recently.'
'Did he leave her much.'
'Two or three times a week.'

*   *   *

Himself is waltzing home absolutely scuttered and happy in the knowledge that he has another half naggin bottle of whiskey hidden in d'arse pocket of his trouser. He stumbles and falls flat on his back. As he gets up slowly he feels a trickle down the back of his leg.

'My God!' sez he, 'I only hope it's blood.'

*   *   *

'I saw a lorry man travel the length of O'Connell Street today on the footpath and he didn't even bat an eyelid.'

'How did he get away with that?'

'He was walking.'

* * *

I wouldn't say that Jemser was mean but there are times when you wouldn't know whether he was bitin' his nails or suckin' a butt.

* * *

Himself arrives home fluthered. It is nearly one in the morning. Herself calls down, 'Is that you, Harry?'

'Yes, dear.'

'What time is it?'

'It's getting on for midnight.'

Just then the cuckoo clock in the hall struck one and Harry had to cuckoo eleven times more.

* * *

'How can you tell the age of a frozen chicken?'

'By the teeth.'

'Come off it, chickens have no teeth.'

'You have.'

* * *

Outside Heuston railway station a little oul' fella approaches a Franciscan carrying a huge suitcase and sez, 'Can I carry your case, father?' The Franciscan agreed and the poor joxer really earns his anticipated reward as he struggles down along the quays with it behind the priest. When they reach Adam and Eve's at Merchant's Quay, the priest turns to his porter:

'You know that we Franciscans have no money — but do you take a drink?'

'Oh, yes, father,' sez the oul' fella.

'Well come inside,' sez the Franciscan, 'and I'll give you the pledge.'

* * *

'Give us a mouse trap in a roaring hurry. I've to catch a bus.'

'I'm sorry, missus, but we've none that size.'

* * *

'Wait till I tell yez, lads. I got the helluva fright last night.'

'I know, I saw you with her.'

* * *

'Why did Hanna leave the job?'
'Illness.'
'Was it serious?'
'Yes. The boss got sick of her.'

* * *

'Our family,' said the Dublin man, 'was so poor that my sister was made in Hong Kong.'

* * *

A fisherman calls on his local fishmonger on his way home from a blank days fishing.

'Throw me five mackerel and a cod,' sez he to the fish merchant.

'Why should I throw them?' sez the fish merchant.

'I want to be able to say to the wife that I caught them.'

* * *

Matty had been out with the boys all evening and ended up at the local carnival, sloshed. He wandered over to the rifle range, picked up a gun and by some quirk of fate hit the bull's eye with his first shot. The attendant presented him with a prize for his marksmanship — a small tortoise — and he wandered off.

Half-an-hour later he was back again and repeated the performance by scoring another bull's eye. The attendant recognising him says: 'And what would you like this time — a teddy bear or a glass jug?'

'Neither,' sez Matty. 'Give us another of those crusty meat pies.'

* * *

WATER BAILIFF: 'Don't you know that fishing is prohibited here!'
POTENTIAL POACHER: 'Fishing? I'm only trying to teach this poor worm to swim.'

* * *

BIRD FANCIER: 'You sold me this canary yesterday.'
PET-SHOP MAN: 'Well?'
BIRD FANCIER: 'Well it's lame!'
PET-SHOP MAN: 'What do you want — a singer or a dancer?'

* * *

Overheard in Dublin shop:
WOMAN: 'Do you keep bananas?'
SHOP-OWNER: 'No, madam, we sell them.'
WOMAN: 'Well you can keep the ones I was going to buy.'

* * *

Dublin man has bad cut on his forehead. Corkman asks him how he got it.

DUBLINER: 'I bit myself.'

CORKMAN: 'How the hell could you bite yourself on your forehead?'

DUBLINER: 'I stood on a chair.'

*   *   *

The parish priest was admiring the old lady's parrot.

'Pull his right leg.' said the old lady.

The parish priest did as she asked and the parrot recited the *Our Father*.

'Now pull his left leg,' said the lady.

This time the parrot said the *Hail Mary*.

'What will happen if I pull both legs together?' joked the parish priest.

'I'll fall on my arse, y'eejit,' said the parrot.

*   *   *

MAN IN RESTAURANT: 'Waitress! My egg is bad.'

WAITRESS: 'Don't blame me, sir, I only laid the table.'

*   *   *

'I can see you're run-down,' said the doctor.

'How?' said the patient.

'By the tyre-marks on your chest.'

*   *   *

MAN: 'I dreamt last night I was eating spaghetti and when I woke up I found I'd eaten half the pillow.'

WIFE: 'And how are you feeling now?'

MAN: 'A little down in the mouth.'

*   *   *

Seal skins make the best pampooties. Banana skins make the best slippers.

*   *   *

The pilgrim arrived home from Lourdes and was being checked out at the Customs.

'What's that?' said the Customs' Officer pointing to a bottle in her case.

'Nothing but a bottle of Lourdes water.'

The official opened the bottle, tasted it and said, 'Madam, that is gin.'

'My God,' said the pilgrim, 'a miracle already.'

*   *   *

There was the story of the Dublin man who used to be a brilliant tap-dancer but had to give it up. It appears that he kept falling into the sink.

* * *

WOMAN: 'Give me two lamb chops and make them lean.'
BUTCHER: 'Certainly, mam. Which way?'

* * *

DOCTOR (on second visit to patient): 'I can see a great improvement. You are coughing much more easily this morning.'
PATIENT: 'I should be. I've been up all the night practising.'

* * *

TOURIST: 'Can you tell me where College Green is?'
GARDA (with huge feet): 'I'm standing on it.'
TOURIST: 'No wonder I couldn't find it.'

* * *

DINER: 'What sort of bird is this?'
WAITER: 'A wood pigeon, sir.'
DINER: 'So I thought. Bring me a saw!'

* * *

GARDA: 'Have you permission to play your fiddle in Grafton Street?'
MUSICIAN: 'No, officer.'
GARDA: 'In that case I must ask you to accompany me.'
MUSICIAN: 'Certainly. And what are you going to sing?'

* * *

'The feud between Harry and Mick is over.'
'Did they bury the hatchet?'
'No. They buried Mick.'

* * *

LADY: 'I'd like a pair of crocodile shoes, please.'
SALESMAN: 'Certainly. What size does your crocodile take?'

* * *

Rᴇᴄᴋʟᴇss BARBER: 'Do you want anything on your face when I've finished?'

NERVOUS CUSTOMER: 'Yes . . . you might leave me my nose.'

* * *

Tᴡᴏ Ringsend sailors were shipwrecked on a desert island.

'Yeh needn't be nervous,' said the first sailor looking at the dancing natives, 'they're only singing a welcome.'

'Welcome my eye,' said the second, 'they're saying grace.'

* * *

Dɪɴᴇʀ: 'Call me the manager. I've never seen anything as tough as this steak.'

WAITER: 'You will if I call the manager.'

* * *

Hᴇ had just been knocked down by a car in Henry Street and a crowd had gathered around him.

'Where am I?' he asked, as he came to.

'Here y'are, mister,' sez a gawking hawker, 'the very thing — a map of Dublin for 10p.'

* * *

CUSTOMER: 'Is this spray good for green fly?'
SHOPKEEPER: 'I'm afraid not, ma'am. It kills them stone dead.'

*　*　*

A man in Drumcondra was training a dog in his back garden. At last when he thought the animal was ready for a trial he got a rabbit. He let the rabbit out on the road and the dog out after it. Ten minutes later a Whitehall man came by on a bicycle, looking very excited.

'Have you seen a rabbit and a dog out the road?' asked the dog fancier.

'Yes,' said the man. 'The best race I've seen in years. When they passed me the dog was leading by five yards.'

*　*　*

Cork Celtic came up to play in Daly-mount towards the end of the season.
CORK MANAGER (inspecting the pitch): 'There's not much grass on that pitch.'
GROUNDSMAN: 'Did yez come to graze or play football?'

*　*　*

Two patients in the doctor's waiting room. One turns to the other and says, 'I'm achin' from neuritis.'

The other replied: 'And I'm O'Mahony from Cork.'

* * *

CUSTOMER: 'A bottle of sauce, please.'
SHOPKEEPER: 'HP?'
CUSTOMER: 'No. I'll pay cash.'

* * *

A large loud Englishwoman came up to a garda in O'Connell Street.

'I say, constable,' sez she, 'could you see me across the street?'

The garda replied: 'I could see you, ma'am, at the other end of the town.'

* * *

YOUNG FELLA: 'Tell us a ghost story, Mrs Hinchy.'
MRS HINCHY: 'How do you know that I know any ghost stories?'
YOUNG FELLA: 'I heard me da say that you give him the creeps.'

* * *

LANDLADY: 'Can you explain how these empty bottles got into your room?'
U.C.D. STUDENT: 'For the life of me I can't. I never bought an empty bottle in my life.'

* * *

SOCIAL WORKER: 'And have you lived all your life in Dublin, Mr Murphy?'
MR MURPHY: 'No. Not yet.'

* * *

MAN IN PUB: 'And when I was in Africa, one morning early I shot a lion in my pyjamas.'
SECOND MAN IN PUB: 'How did he get in there?'

* * *

Connolly was in Mountjoy. Shifty went to see him.
SHIFTY: 'How long are you in for?'
CONNOLLY: 'Six months.'
SHIFTY: 'What's the charge?'
CONNOLLY: 'None at all. Everything's free.'

* * *

A man called at the Department of Posts and Telegraphs and presented the telephone supervisor with a bouquet of flowers.

'This is for your telephonists,' he said.

'Thank you,' said the supervisor, 'they'll be ever so flattered.'

'Flattered be damned,' said the man, 'I thought they were all dead.'

*　　*　　*

PATIENT: 'Is it serious, doctor?'
DOCTOR: 'No. No. But I wouldn't buy any new long-playing records, if I were you.'

*　　*　　*

The class was being questioned on the Prodigal Son's return.

'And who was sorry when the Prodigal Son returned?' asked the teacher.

'The fatted calf,' replied the little boy.

*　　*　　*

A Dublin man decided to take a trip to the continent. As he boarded the plane at Dublin airport a little red truck came along and filled the plane with fuel. They landed at London and out came a little red truck and refuelled the plane immediately. When they landed in Paris a little red truck was waiting for them and filled the plane once more. The pilot walked down through the passengers and, looking at his watch, said to the Dubliner: 'We're making excellent time today.'

'Maybe y'are,' said the Dubliner, 'but that little red truck is beatin' yeh to it all the time.'

* * *

The ragman knocks on the door of a Mount Merrion house.
'Got any old clothes, scrap or news-papers, Mister?'
MAN OF THE HOUSE: 'My good man, the wife's away and I wouldn't know anything about such things.'
RAGMAN: 'Then any chance you'd have a few empty bottles?'

* * *

WOMAN: 'A pound of apples, please.'
SHOPKEEPER: 'Will you take Granny Smith's?'
WOMAN: 'No. I can barely carry me own.'

* * *

JOXER: 'Give us a packet of Rinso. I want to wash the budgie.'
SHOPKEEPER: 'Oh, but you can't wash a budgie in Rinso. It will kill the budgie.'
JOXER: 'Give us the Rinso.'
SHOPKEEPER: 'Right, sir, but don't say I didn't warn you.'
Joxer leaves the shop and returns a fortnight later.
SHOPKEEPER: 'Well, how's the budgie?'
JOXER: 'The budgie? Oh, the budgie's dead.'
SHOPKEEPER: 'I warned you that the Rinso would kill the budgie.'
JOXER: 'Oh, the Rinso was game ball. I think it was the mangle that done it.'

* * *

Tourist rolls down car window in O'Connell Street and shouts to newspaper boy, 'Say, which way to Stephen's Green?'

'I dunno,' sez the newspaper seller.

'Well then, how do you get to Rathmines?' sez the tourist.

'I dunno,' sez the young lad.

'Don't you know anything?' sez the irritable tourist.

'Well, I'll tell ye one thing,' sez the newspaper seller, 'I'm not lost.'

* * *

'And what brings you here?' said the friendly psychiatrist to the little old lady.

'They say I'm mad because I like pancakes,' said the little lady.

'Why, that's no reason. I love pancakes myself,' said the psychiatrist.

'You must come to tea,' said the little lady, 'I've trunks full of them.'

* * *

The religious instruction class was discussing 'death'.

JIMMY: 'My uncle knew to the hour and the minute when he was going to die.'

TEACHER: 'And how did he know that, Jimmy?'

JIMMY: 'The judge told him.'

*   *   *

The circus is coming to town, in by Liffey Junction. The elephants, all four of them, walk in traditional fashion, each one grasping with his trunk the tail of the elephant in front of him. They reach the level-crossing and cross it safely, almost. A train comes along, knocks down and kills the last elephant. In due course the circus bill comes with the damages including the loss of four elephants. 'But we only killed one elephant,' said a spokesman.

'Yes,' said the circus owner, 'but you tore d'arse out of the other three.'

*   *   *

A railway station-master thought he'd get married on the cheap. Trains being few and far between he decided he would run the ceremony and reception in the room over the ticket office. During the celebrations the floor collapsed and all were killed.

The moral: Do not marry above your station.

* * *

A man's hat came floating down the river Tolka. As it passed the fisherman on the bank he was amazed to see it rise and reveal a face underneath.

'Am I right for Fairview?' asked a voice.

'Straight on down,' said the fisherman.

'Thanks,' said the voice and the hat went floating down the river once more.

The fisherman shouted after it, 'It's a long, long way down.'

The hat rose once more and the voice said, 'That's all right, I'm on me brother's bike.'

* * *

MOTHER: 'Why should you be kept in school, son, because another boy was smoking in class?'
SON: 'I'm the one that set him alight, mum.'

*   *   *

Nervous little man to attendant on roof of Liberty Hall: 'Do people fall off the roof often?'

'No, sir. Only the once,' said the attendant.

*   *   *

DUBLINER: 'Give us a return ticket.'
CLERK: 'Where to?'
DUBLINER: 'Back here, of course.'

*   *   *

Small boy always wondered where the sun went at night. So much so that he sat in his window looking out long after the sun had gone down. He stayed there all night. The following morning it dawned on him.

*   *   *

FIRST FOOTBALL FAN: 'Why do you call that goalkeeper Cinderella?'
SECOND FOOTBALL FAN: 'Because more often than not he misses the ball.'

* * *

JUSTICE TO DOLLY-BIRD IN COURT: 'And what gear were you in when the garda stopped your car?'
DOLLY-BIRD: 'Well, actually, I was wearing this grey tweed suit with white boots and . . .'

* * *

'Why is it,' said the irritable lady customer, 'that I never get what I look for in this shop?'

'Maybe,' said the assistant, 'because we are too polite.'

* * *

OLD LADY: 'My poor, poor man. I suppose you have had many trials in your life.'
TRAMP: 'Yes ma'am, but only one conviction.'

* * *

'I think Granny needs glasses.'

'Why do you say that?'

'She's out in the kitchen sitting in front of the washing machine.'

'What's wrong with that?'

'Nothing, only she was watching Dad's long underwear going round and round and she's shouting, "The best wrestling I've seen on the telly in ages".'

* * *

A little old man was discovered going round and round in the revolving door of the G.P.O.

'Are you all right?' asked the official.

'Yes,' said the absent-minded wee man, 'but I can't remember whether I was on my way in or my way out.'

* * *

FIRST SMALL BOY: 'There's a fella lives on our road who used work in the circus putting his right arm into the lion's mouth.'

SECOND SMALL BOY: 'What's his name?'

FIRST SMALL BOY: 'I dunno, but we all call him "Lefty".'

* * *

A young innocent-looking lad was at his first dance in a Dublin ballroom. In his innocence he walks up to a girl who seems to have come for more than the dancing.

'I'm sorry,' says she, 'but I never dance with a child.'

'I beg your pardon,' said the young man, 'I didn't notice your condition.'

* * *

MAN: 'I want you to remove my wife's tonsils one of these days.'
DOCTOR: 'My good man, I removed them five years ago. You've never heard of a woman having two sets of tonsils have you?'
MAN: 'No, but you've heard of a man having two wives, haven't you?'

* * *

JOHNER: 'I'm not so sure of one word in the crossword.'
WACKER: 'What's the clue?'
JOHNER: 'A four-letter word ending in IT meaning substance found in the bottom of a bird-cage.'
WACKER: 'Grit.'
JOHNER: 'Give us the rubber.'

* * *

A good-livin' Dublin woman was down the country on her holidays and met this young fella leading a dangerous-looking bull.

'Where are you going with the bull?' she asked the culchie.

'He's going to service a cow down the road,' said the young fella.

'Couldn't your father do that?' asked the woman.

'No,' said the young fella, 'it's got to be the bull.'

* * *

HIMSELF: 'You're a smashin' dancer.'
HERSELF: 'I wish I could say the same for you.'
HIMSELF: 'You could if you were as big a liar as me.'

* * *

The parish priest rang the health board office and reported that there was a dead donkey outside his house.

'But I thought you looked after the dead,' quipped the clerk.

'We do,' said the P.P. 'but only after we have contacted the relatives.'

* * *

Would the people of Sandymount's manners improve if they had a refinery in the bay?

* * *

In the days of the Capitol Theatre's stage show Jack Kirwan was the resident comedian for many years. One night during a performance a member of the audience offered him the ultimate in show-biz insults by throwing a penny on the stage. Without batting an eyelid Jack walked over, picked up the penny and offered it back to the thrower.

'Here,' sez Jack, 'don't be throwing away your overtime like that.'

* * *

On another occasion Jack was hauled up to the manager's office for something he'd done.

When he sat down the manager noticed a butt of a cigarette on the carpet under Kirwan's chair.

'Is that your butt?' roared the manager.

'No,' says Kirwan, 'you saw it first.'

* * *

PATIENT: 'I've lost my memory.'
DOCTOR: 'When did it happen.'
PATIENT: 'When did what happen?'

*   *   *

An old lady was bashed over the head with a fiddle and her purse stolen near the College of Music. Two men are helping the police with their enquiries. It is expected that they will be charged with robbery with violins.

*   *   *

The standard of driving is such on the new dual carriageway at Belfield that the city fathers are thinking of naming it the Ben Hur Memorial Road.

*   *   *

'Our electric toaster is not so much a pop-up affair but rather a Red Indian model.'
'What do you mean?'
'It sends up smoke signals.'

*   *   *

A woman walks up Moore Street with two ducks in an orange crate.

'Are you goin' to a party?' shouts her friend Mary.

'What made you think that?' says the woman.

'Where else,' says Mary, 'would you be going with a box of quackers?'

* * *

A DEFINITION OF PROBATE: A man walking up Hatch Street with a ten pound note sticking out of his fly.

* * *

BALLYBRACK MAN: 'That's a fierce lump on yer head, Mick. What gave it to you?'
MICK: 'Mushroom soup.'
BALLYBRACK MAN: 'How could mushroom soup cause a lump like that?'
MICK: 'It was in a tin.'

* * *

Two fellas decided to go to a fancy dress party dressed as a cow. Halfway there the car broke down and they had to walk so they took a shortcut across the fields. To get used to their costume Mick donned the back legs and Pat the front half of the cow. They were only getting used to their roles when Pat shouts, 'Mick, there's a bull coming. What'll I do?'

Mick, from behind says: 'Brace yourself.'

*   *   *

'He's the most striking man I've met in years.'
'Is he really that good-looking.'
'No, he's a bus conductor.'

*   *   *

WIFE: 'Go out and water the garden, dear.'
HUSBAND: 'But it is raining, dear.'
WIFE: 'Well, put on your raincoat.'

*   *   *

A Dublin shopkeeper was explaining to a stranger: 'I've got a silver medal for swimming, four for football, and three for hurling. I've two cups for boxing and some golfing prizes.'

'My, you must be a fantastic athlete.'

'Not really — I run a pawnshop.'

* * *

A woman lives near us and she suffers from marital thrombosis — she is married to a clot.

* * *

'I'm a life-guard in an automatic car-wash.'

'Did you ever have to rescue anyone?'

'Every day.'

'How's that?'

'Well, we get a lot of culchies in on motor-bikes.'

* * *

An old maid in a down-town hotel rings for the manager.

'It's a disgrace,' she says to him. 'I looked out my window and saw this man taking a bath in a room across from mine.'

The manager came up and looked out the window.

'But, madam,' says he, 'I can only see the top of that man's head.'

'Here,' said the old maid, 'you just stand on that table.'

* * *

A Dublin coal merchant who became a politician was speaking on an election platform. A hard chaw in the crowd was giving him a tough time with cat-calls and insinuations of his party's skullduggery. Finally, his patience broke.

'Right,' said the politician, 'if it's dirt you want it's dirt you'll get.'

'Yes,' said the hard chaw, 'at twenty pound a ton.'

* * *

A very worried-looking man knocked on Mrs Murphy's door.

'I'm very sorry, Mrs,' said the man, 'I've just run over your dog. I'd like to replace it.'

'That's all right, Cúchullainn,' said Mrs Murphy. 'Your bowl is in the garage.'

*　*　*

There once was a man who bought a rubber trumpet — just to play in a rubber band.

*　*　*

Nothing would do the Irish business tycoon but to buy a tiny seaplane and fly it himself. First time out his instructor noticed he was about to land it at Dublin Airport.

'Excuse me, sir,' said the instructor, 'but would it not be better to land on the water at Clontarf?'

'Of course,' said the tycoon gruffly, and headed for Clontarf.

He landed the plane successfully and turned to the instructor.

'You didn't think I was going to land on the ground, did you!' said he. He then opened the door of the plane and stepped out into the sea.

*　*　*

Miko Gill, budding Dublin author, was having trouble in finding his rent. He explained to his landlady: 'But don't you realise that one day there'll be a plaque on this house saying "Miko Gill lived here".'

'If you don't pay your rent,' said the landlady, 'they can start putting up that plaque tomorrow.'

* * *

A Dublin supporter was up in court for assaulting a culchie.

'I was only trying to cure him,' explained the Dub.

'Cure him of what?' asked the judge.

'I thought he had water on the brain,' said the accused.

'And what did you do for him in the circumstances?' enquired the judge.

'Like I said to the garda,' the Dubliner replied, 'I gave him a few taps on the head.'

* * *

A Dublin man went into the G.P.O. to make a complaint.

'I got a letter by post this morning that was posted in Kilkenny five days ago,' said the man.

'Well?' said the Department of Posts & Telegraphs' spokesman.

'Why,' said the outraged Dubliner, 'over a hundred and fifty years ago it only took ten hours from Kilkenny to Dublin by horse-drawn coach.'

'All right,' said the spokesman, 'but you must realise that those horses are now way past their best.'

* * *

'Waiter, you've got your thumb on the fish,' said the angry diner to the man serving his meal.

'Course I have sir,' said the waiter. 'I don't want it to jump on the floor again.'

* * *

TRINITY GRADUATE: 'I wonder if you remember me? Years ago you asked me to marry you.'

ABSENT-MINDED PROFESSOR: 'And did you?'

* * *